Summr

Mindset

By: Carol S Dweck

Proudly Brought to you by:

Legal & Disclaimer

Legal & Disclaimer

The information contained in this book is not designed to
replace or take the place of any form of medicine or
professional medical advice. The information in this book has
been provided for educational and entertainment purposes
only.

The information contained in this book has been compiled
from sources deemed reliable, and it is accurate to the best of
the Author's knowledge; however, the Author cannot
guarantee its accuracy and validity and cannot be held liable
for any errors or omissions. Changes are periodically made to
this book. You must consult your doctor or get professional
medical advice before using any of the suggested remedies,
techniques, or information in this book. Images used in this
book is not the same as of that of the actual book. This is a

Table of Contents

FREE BONUSES

<u>P.S. Is it okay if we overdeliver?</u>

Here at Readtrepreneur Publishing, we believe in overdelivering way beyond our reader's expectations. Is it okay if we overdeliver?

Here's the deal, we're going to give you an extremely condensed PDF summary of the book which you've just read and much more...

What's the catch? We need to trust you... You see, we want to overdeliver and in order for us to do that, we've to trust our reader to keep this bonus a secret to themselves? Why? Because we don't want people to be getting our exclusive PDF summaries even without buying our books itself. Unethical, right?

Ok. Are you ready?

Firstly, remember that your book is code: **"READ59"**.

Next, visit this link: <u>http://bit.ly/exclusivepdfs</u>

Everything else will be self explanatory after you've visited: <u>http://bit.ly/exclusivepdfs</u>.

We hope you'll enjoy our free bonuses as much as we enjoyed preparing it for you!

The Book at a Glance

This book is a summary of the groundbreaking book, "Mindset: The New Psychology of Success" by Carol S. Dweck.

In this book, you will learn various techniques to help you reap the power of your mind. You'll learn:

- ✓ Why people are different from one another

- ✓ The two mindsets – what they are and their pros and cons

- ✓ The truth about your self-insight

- ✓ What is success

- ✓ How your mindset can change the meaning of effort and failure

- ✓ The danger of praising your child

- ✓ How to take charge of your success

- ✓ What is a growth mindset and how to develop it

- ✓ How to be a good negotiator

- ✓ How to frame your mindset to achieve relationship success

- ✓ How to deal with bullies

- ✓ How to change your mindset

- ✓ Why people do not want to change

- ✓ How to change your child's mindset

- ✓ The relationship between willpower and mindset

This book will help you develop the type of mindset you need to reach your goals and succeed in all areas of your life.

In the first chapter, you will discover why people are different from one another. You will get an overview of the two mindsets.

In the second chapter, you will learn how your mindset defines the meaning of effort or failure. You will learn that success is not at all about winning, but is about making an effort.

The third chapter is primarily about the perils of positive and negative labels. We will discuss the reasons why you should not praise your child for being brilliant or smart.

The fourth chapter is about sports. You'll learn why Michael Jordan was a superstar. It also contains real sports stories to help you identify the secret of success in sports.

The fifth chapter is about business and how a leader's mindset can lead to the growth or downfall of the enterprise.

In the sixth chapter, we will discuss why some people are luckier in love than others. We will also discuss the mindset of bullies.

In the seventh chapter, you'll learn the main difference between horrible and great teachers.

In the eighth chapter, you will learn how you can change your mindset and that of your child. You'll learn how to use your mindset to improve various areas of your life – health, finances and career.

You are your thoughts. You are your beliefs. It is time to change them, so you can change your life.

Chapter 1: The Mindsets

When Carol was still a young researcher, she was obsessed with studying how people cope with failure. She watched how children deal with problems and difficult puzzles. This was a time when she saw something extraordinary and expected. Most of these kids love the challenge. She never encountered people who actually loved failure. Carol felt that these kids knew something she did not. That's when she decided to understand the kind of mindset that could transform failure and challenges into a gift.

These kids know that human intellect is something that can be developed through constant effort, and is the reason they get smarter over time. But, not all people are like this. Most think that intellect or human qualities are carved in stone. In the next sections of this book, you'll learn why people differ. You'll also learn about the two mindsets and how they can shape your reality.

Why do People Differ?

People think and act differently. That's old news. But, why do people differ? Why are some people more moral than others? Why are some people smarter than others?

Many people think that our intelligence depends on the physical makeup of our brains – the bumps and shape of the skull, the size of the organ, and genes. But a number of experts now believe that experience, training, and environment contribute to intelligence.

In fact, Alfred Binet (the creator of the IQ test) is a strong believer that intelligence is something that can be developed. He created the IQ test to identify children who were not learning in the public school system of Paris at that time. The test was designed to develop new learning methods and not determine intelligence.

Binet knew that children's intelligence differs and that some kids are really smarter than others. But, he also knew that education and training can change a person's intelligence.

So, who's right? Is intelligence something we inherit or that we can develop? Well, scientists now believe it can be both. Genes play an important role in its development. Effort and training can also significantly increase one's intelligence over time. To use Binet's words, "it's not always the ones who start out to be the smartest, end up becoming the smartest."

What Does all This Mean for You? The Two Mindsets

Dr. Carol Dweck's twenty-year research shows that beliefs about yourself affect how your life turns out. It determines your chances of achieving the things that are important to you. But, how does this happen? How can a belief transform your life? Before we discuss it, let's get to know the two mindsets – the Fixed Mindset and the Growth Mindset.

1. The Fixed Mindset

When you have a fixed mindset, you believe that your skills and abilities are carved in stone. This mindset cultivates a strong need to prove yourself again and again.

Many people are trained to have a fixed mindset at a very early age. In fact, most teachers train their students to adopt this kind of mindset – you're either smart or dumb. Thus, people with this mindset strive to be aces on tests and look smart all the time.

When fixed mindset people fail, they think they're a failure and a loser. They feel worthless. To put it simply, they think that what happens to them is a reflection of their worth and competence.

So, are people with fixed mindset pessimists or do they just have low self-esteem? The answer is no. Fixed mindset people are optimistic and confident when they are not dealing with failure.

People with a fixed mindset deal with failure by doing nothing, staying in bed, listening to music all day, crying or picking a fight with someone.

2. Growth Mindset

When you have a growth mindset, you believe that the cards you're dealt are just the starting point of your development. People with a growth mindset believe that everyone has an unknown potential. They believe that you cannot foresee what one can accomplish through years of training, effort and hard work.

Do you know that Charles Darwin and Leo Tolstoy were just ordinary children when growing up? There's nothing special about them. Ben Hogan, a gifted golfer, was clumsy and had poor motor skills when he was a child. The great actress, Geraldine Page, was once asked to quit show business because of her lack of talent.

Growth mindset people see failure as an opportunity to work harder, learn something new and be better. When they fail in an exam, they just study harder. They do not mope around and feel sorry for themselves: they take action and grab life by the balls.

People with a fixed mindset tend to deny their deficiencies instead of working to overcome them. People with a growth mindset, on the other hand, embrace their failures and inadequacies. They believe that intelligence can be developed and this creates an intense interest in learning.

So, What's New?

The growth mindset is not a novel idea. We have long known the importance of persistence, perseverance, hard work and taking risks. But, as you begin to understand the two mindsets, you'll see how your beliefs influence your effort and the courage to take risks. You will now comprehend how your mindset influences your thoughts, decisions, behaviors and actions. This book will help you reorient your beliefs, so you will see the value of hard work and education through a different lens.

Self-Insight: Who has Accurate Views of Their Assets and Limitations?

Studies show that most people have inaccurate views of their abilities and talents. But, fixed minded people are those who have inaccurate views of their talents. People with a growth mindset have surprisingly accurate views of their talents and abilities.

If you believe you have the capacity to develop your abilities, you're more likely to accurately assess your current ones. You accept accurate information about your talents and use this to learn more and be better. Howard Gardner wrote in "Extraordinary Minds" that insanely successful individuals have a talent for correctly identifying their strengths and weaknesses. And oddly enough, people with a growth mindset have this talent.

What's in Store?

One of the most amazing things about exceptional people is that they have a talent for transforming problems and failures into future wins and successes simply because they exhibit resilience and perseverance. But, how can beliefs lead to success? In the next chapters, you will discover how your mindset can help you achieve more in life and how it affects your performance in sports, school, work and relationships.

Major Points

- ✓ Intelligence is not a fixed ability. It is something you can acquire over time.

- ✓ All human beings have the capacity to learn new things and increase their intelligence over time.

- ✓ Your beliefs can lead to success.

Chapter 2: Inside the Mindsets

As mentioned, there are two types of mindsets. The first one, the fixed mindset, pushes you to prove and validate yourself. The second one, the growth mindset, pushes you to develop yourself.

When you have a fixed mindset, you see getting fired or rejected as a sign that you're not smart or good enough. You see failure as a problematic situation like losing a game, losing your business, or failing a college course.

When you have a growth mindset, you see failure as not making any strides or not reaching your full potential. You believe that effort makes you talented and smart. Both mindsets are a collection of powerful beliefs. But, the good news is, you have a choice. You can choose to adopt a fixed or a growth mindset. The next sections of this book will help you decide which to adopt.

Is Success About Learning – Or Proving You're Smart?

Success is not about proving you are better than others. It is about learning and giving your best effort. In the end, intelligence is something you have to work for.

The CEO Disease

A lot of people want to be seen as perfect. This behavior is aptly named the "CEO disease." Former Chrysler Motors executive, Lee Iacocca, had a bad case of this disease. He kept on bringing the same car models (with just minor changes) over and over while his Japanese competitors were putting innovative cars on the market. Not long after, the company had to file for bankruptcy.

Many CEOs pretend they don't have shortcomings. They surround themselves with acolytes who worship them and exile their critics. Most do not see the value of learning new skills or improving themselves.

Not everyone develops this disease. In fact, there are a number of successful and powerful leaders who confront their failures and weaknesses on a regular basis.

Mindsets Change the Meaning of Failure

The Martins love their son, Robert. They always think he's better than other kids. Then, when he was three, Robert did the unforgivable – he did not get into the best pre-school in NYC. Suddenly, his parents treated him differently. At this young age, he already felt like a loser and a failure. Unfortunately, a lot of people have had the same fate as Robert.

Your mindset defines the meaning of failure. Growth mindset people see setbacks as a painful experience, but they also see it as an opportunity to grow and be better. When they make a mistake, they quickly pick themselves up and put in more effort. They are brave enough to admit their mistakes and use them to be a better player, worker, partner, student, etc.

Fixed mindset people see failure as a permanent, haunting and traumatic experience. To illustrate this point, let's look at the case of a great French chef named Bernard Loiseau. He popularized cream sauces. In 2003, he committed suicide after rumors circulated that he would lose stars in the prestigious Guide Michelin. He did not; but the fear of failure led him to end his life. Loiseau has a fixed mindset and he associated losing Michelin stars with being a "has been" and a failure.

You'd be surprised what people with a fixed mindset consider as a failure. They consider other people's success as their failure. This is the reason why they are more prone to depression.

When fixed mindset people fail, they repair their self-esteem, not their failure. Instead of learning from their mistakes, they look for people who are worse off than they so they feel good about themselves. For example, if they get low test scores, they'll look for people who have lower scores. They also fix their self-esteem by making excuses or blaming others. When they're faced with challenges, they just give up: they don't take action to solve their problems.

People with a growth mindset define failure differently. They see it as a challenge and an opportunity to acquire new knowledge and skills. When they are faced with failure, they become more determined and persistent. They believe their qualities can be developed and do not allow failure to define them. They believe there are different paths to success, so they do not waste their time crying over spilled milk.

For fixed mindset people, success is about being better than others. It is about being smarter or more gifted than others. People with a growth mindset believe that success is being your best self and putting forth your best effort.

Mindsets Change the Meaning of Effort

We live in a society where we celebrate what Malcolm Gladwell calls "effortless accomplishment." We have the fantasy that Michael Jordan was born dribbling and Picasso was already painting before he could learn to talk. Let's face it, we live in a society with a fixed mindset where we prefer effortless success and perfection. Most of us believe that effort is only for people with a lack of talent and intelligence. We believe that effort reduces us and makes us less smart, talented or gifted.

But, people with a growth mindset think differently. They know that even geniuses have to work hard to get where they are. They believe that effort is that fire that turns skills into achievement.

Questions and Answers

Question: If fixed mindset people believe their talents are fixed and that they are talented or smart, why do they have to keep proving themselves?

This is because we face new and larger demons every day. For example, you may have received exceptional grades in high school, but college is a different story. You may be good enough to write for a tabloid, but not good enough to write for the New York Times.

Question: Can you change your mindset?

Yes, you can. When you are aware of the two mindsets, you can train your mind to think differently. If you currently have a fixed mindset, you can always adopt a growth mindset.

Question: Can I have both mindsets?

Yes. In fact, many people have elements of both mindsets. Also, most people can have different mindsets in various areas of their lives. For example, you can have fixed artistic skills, but your physical attributes or cognitive abilities can be developed.

Question: When people fail, is it entirely their fault?

No. Effort is important, but it's not the only key to success. Resources and external opportunities play an important role. People with rich parents can take more risk and are constantly exposed to many opportunities--the reason why they are more likely to succeed.

Question: I know a lot of people who are workaholics. They are always trying to prove how smart they are. How does this fit with the idea that people with a fixed mindset do not exert effort?

Most of the time, people with a fixed mindset prefer effortless success; but, there are a number of powerful people with such a mindset. In fact, a lot of industry leaders have one.

Question: I know what my talent is and I like I have a fixed mindset. Why would I give that up?

If you like having a fixed mindset, you can always keep it. You have a choice. This book merely defines the two mindsets and the type of outcomes they create.

Question: Can you change everything about who you are?

The growth mindset operates under the premise that skills can be acquired. But, there are some things that you cannot change – preferences, principles, etc. Also, you do not have to change everything possible. It's okay to accept your imperfections, especially those that do not have the power to destroy your life or other people's lives.

Question: Is it true that people with a fixed mindset simply lack self-confidence or self-esteem?

No. People with fixed mindset and those with a growth mindset usually have the same level of confidence in the beginning. But, because people with a growth mindset exert effort to hone their skills, their confidence increases over time.

Major Points

✓ Growth mindset people do not only seek challenge; they stretch themselves to rise above it. You see this often in the world of sports.

✓ People with a fixed mindset thrive only when they feel safe. They thrive when they are in their comfort zones. When things get challenging, they just give up.

✓ Growth mindset people feel they're smart when they are learning. People with a fixed mindset feel smart when they don't make mistakes.

✓ Becoming is better than being.

✓ People with a fixed mindset are afraid of admitting their mistakes. Growth mindset people are not afraid to lose face by admitting their shortcomings.

✓ Fixed mindset people prefer instant success over learning and growing. They are constantly trying to prove they are superior and special. They want to feel they are better than others. They are entitled.

✓ People with a fixed mindset think that putting in effort is an admission of weakness. They think that effort is for less talented human beings.

Chapter 3: The Truth About Ability and Accomplishment

Many people thought that Thomas Edison was a loner, genius and an unworldly sage. They used to think that he discovered the light bulb all by himself. But, that's far from the truth. He had a large team of glassblowers, engineers, mathematicians, and physicists. In fact, he had a state-of-the-art laboratory and was a smart and shrewd entrepreneur.

Edison knew how to publicize himself. He was a genius, but he was not born that way. He was quite ordinary as a kid. What set him apart from other people was his drive and growth mindset. He always looked for new challenges.

Mozart is a bit similar to Edison. He worked hard for ten years before he produced something impressive.

Mindset and School Achievement

Carol Dweck measured a number of student mindsets as they entered high school. You see, the transition to high school is one of the most challenging times young people have to go through. Dr. Dweck's study shows that only the grades of those students with a fixed mindset declined significantly. The students with a growth mindset increased their grades over a period of two years.

Dr. Dweck's researchers asked the students with a fixed mindset to explain their declining school performance. They gave reasons like, "I am bad in math" or "I am stupid". Some blamed their teachers and classmates.

Students with a growth mindset did not complain or blame others. They find junior high challenging, too. But, they said they'd do whatever it takes to succeed and pass every subject.

Unfortunately, most high school students have low effort syndrome. They inflate their egos by not trying, so they can look cool. It's a way to protect themselves from other people's judgment.

For students with a growth mindset, not exerting effort does not make sense. Even when there's a huge possibility of failure, they just kept trying. They mobilize all their resources to learn and be better in school.

Dr. Dweck conducted the same study on students transitioning to college, and the results are pretty much the same. Students with a fixed mindset stop when things get challenging. But, growth mindset college students do not stop reading a book that's difficult to follow. They just read it over and over until they understand it.

Does this mean that anyone can do well in school if only they have the right mindset? Does this mean that all kids are born equal? Well, kids are not born equal. Gifted children really do exist. These children have obsessive interests and extraordinary abilities. Most of these gifted children were born with a special skill or ability. But, what makes them really stand out is their extreme love for challenge and learning. They love demanding activities. They are curious and constantly pursue challenging activities.

A lot of people think that the gift is the ability; but, it's not. The real gift is the curiosity and an intense love for learning new things. The real gift is the obsession.

We all have an interest we can turn into a skill or ability through constant practice. With the right amount of effort, teaching, and a good mindset, anyone can do something they want to do. With the right learning environment, anyone can learn whatever they want to learn.

The renowned teacher, Marva Collins, proved this. She took in a few Chicago children who had learning abilities and treated them like geniuses. She asked these kids to read books like Jane Eyre and A Tale of Two Cities over and over. She taught them to work hard. In just a few years, these kids were smarter than the children attending prestigious schools.

An educational researcher named Benjamin Bloom studied more than a hundred achievers – Olympic athletes, accomplished musicians, neurologists and mathematicians. They were not extraordinary. What is the real key to their success? Well, a combination of commitment, persistence, perseverance, motivation, and support of the people around them.

Is Artistic Ability a Gift?

People usually think that intelligence is something we're born with. This is actually not true. Intelligence is something you can develop in time. But, artistic ability is purely a gift. It's God-given. Although there are components of drawing that can be learned, some special people are born artists. They can draw well even without training. But, those who were not born with artistic abilities can always practice to improve their drawing skills.

The Danger of Praise and Positive Labels

We all think that our parent's praise is good for us. It motivates us. We think it's a fuel that motivates us to do our best; but, positive labels and praises are dangerous. If your parents praised you and constantly told you that you were smart, you'd eventually think that you are smart. And then, when something happens that makes you feel like you're not, you instantly feel like you're a failure: you reject challenging tasks that can potentially hurt your ego.

The danger of praise is that it pushes you to develop a fixed mindset. It pushes you to reject challenging tasks from which you could learn just because you do not want to expose your flaws and hurt your ego. When you tell your kids that they're smart or talented, they'll eventually lie to cover up their failures.

So, should parents not praise their children? They should. But, they should not praise the outcome. They should instead commend the effort. Kids who are commended and praised for their effort seek new and challenging problems. They tend to do well even in difficult situations.

Positive labels are dangerous, but negative labels are also bad. Constant criticism can cause you to give up. It makes you think you are not good enough; it limits your growth. When people tell you you're stupid, you'll be less likely to take on a challenging task because you think you're not good enough.

But, this only happens to people with a fixed mindset. Growth mindset people do not allow negative labels to affect their performance. When someone tells them they are not good enough, they just work harder: they thrive even in threatening environments.

To sum up, both positive and negative labels can mess with your head if you have a fixed mindset. If people tell you that you are smart, you don't take on challenges because you're afraid of losing the label. If people tell you that you're stupid, you don't attempt challenging tasks because you think you're not good enough.

People with growth mindset, on the other hand, do not allow labels to define them. They work hard no matter what.

Grow Your Mindset Tips

- To develop a growth mindset and overcome labels, you need to correctly identify your current one. Do you ever feel that your hero achieved success with minimal effort? If yes, take time to find out the truth.

- Do you label your kids? Remember that labeling is not helpful. Compliment their efforts instead.

- If you ever feel stupid, don't feel sorry for yourself. Get yourself into the growth mindset by thinking about how you can learn and be better.

Major Points

✓ You can learn just about anything if you are in the right learning environment.

✓ Successful people usually grew up as ordinary kids with the extraordinary ability to persist even when faced with failure.

✓ The gift is not the ability. It's the love of learning and persistence. It's the love of challenge.

✓ Having a fixed mindset can limit your achievement because it diminishes the value of effort.

✓ All types of achievement require hard work and effort. This is the reason why people with the growth mindset are more likely to succeed in life.

✓ Artistic ability is a God-given gift. But, there are components of this ability that can be learned through constant practice.

✓ People with a fixed mindset allow both negative and positive labels to mess with their heads. People with a growth mindset, on the other hand, put in effort no matter what other people tell them. They do not allow labels to mess with their heads.

✓ Parents should praise their children's efforts and not the end result. This way, their children will see the value of effort and hard work.

✓ Mindset is more powerful and important than talent.

Chapter 4 - Sports: The Mindset of a Champion

Many believe that athletes are talented and have special gifts. We all think that people who excel in sports are those who move like athletes and act like athletes. They think that athletes are born and not made. But, this is not true. Mindset is everything.

Let's look at the case of Billy Beane. When he was in high school, people thought he would be the next Babe Ruth. He had real talent. But, there's one thing he did not have – the mindset of a winner. He would throw a tantrum the minute something went wrong.

He thought he was talented and his spirit was ruined every time he failed to make it to first base. He had a problem, but he never tried to fix it because he has a classic fixed mindset; natural talent must not ask for help, admit weakness, or make an effort.

Beane was trapped for some time. But his mindset changed when he met another player named Lenny Dykstra. You see,

Lenny did not have Beane's natural ability. What's special about him is that he does not have a concrete concept of failure. So, Dykstra eventually transformed himself into a "gifted" baseball player.

This is when Beane knew that mindset is everything. So, he changed his mindset and became a successful sports executive.

The Idea of the Natural "Character"

A lot of people think that sports superstars are "naturals" born to play basketball or football. But, there are a number of superstars who were not "naturals". Michael Jordan is one of them. When he was in high school, he was removed from the basketball team. He was heart-broken. But, he used his disappointment to work hard. He worked harder than anyone else. He developed a mental toughness that allowed him to thrive in unfavorable circumstances.

Babe Ruth was also not a natural. He was extremely disciplined and loved to practice. He studied the throws of his rival catchers and pitchers. Soon enough, he developed a technique that would distract pitchers and drive the fans wild.

The world of sports glorifies naturals because people usually put a premium on natural skill. They do not appreciate earned ability as much. The truth is, to achieve long-term success in the field of sports, you must have the heart, soul and spirit of a champion. Character and strength, not natural talent, help you reach the top and stay there. People like Mike Tyson reached the pinnacle of sports success. But, they did not stay there.

What is Success?

People with the growth mindset find success in doing their best and improving. This is exactly the same mindset we frequently find in champions. For them, personal success is when you work hard and put in massive effort.

Champions like Mia Hamm and Tiger Woods focus on the amount of effort they exert and not on their victory. They're both hard workers who want to be the best in whatever they do. A lot of people do not want to rehearse; they just want to perform. But, superstars already felt like winners when they are practicing, rehearsing, and putting in their best effort to put on the best show.

What is Failure?

Here's an interesting fact about people with the growth mindset – they find setbacks and failure motivating. They embrace failures and use them as a fuel to succeed in whatever they do.

When Michael Jordan returned to basketball after a long hiatus, the Chicago Bulls were eliminated from the play-offs. Instead of whining, Jordan recognized that he was not as good as before. So, he practiced more than a hundred times to dominate the game again. After that, his team won the NBA championship for three straight seasons.

For people with the growth mindset, failure is informative and a powerful wake-up call. It is a motivation.

Taking Charge of Success

People with the growth mindset take charge of their success in sports. They work harder as they age. They put in more effort and change their game strategy when necessary. They control their motivation, focus, and attention: they take responsibility.

What Does it Mean to be a Star?

What is a star? Does he have to do more than regular players? How do stars like Michael Jordan or Kobe Bryant think?

A respected coach named John Wooden claimed that Michael Jordan was strategically and tactically average. But, what made him special? Why did he win that many championships? Well, one of the best things about Jordan is that he got other players to work as a team.

Athletes with a fixed mindset act like a superstar and not a member of a team. But, real stars say "we" and not "I". They see their teammates as powerful contributors to their greatness and success. The truth is, EVERY SPORT IS A TEAM SPORT. Even if you are involved in "individual sports", you're not going to make it alone. You'll need a team--your coach, assistant, mentor, training/sparring partner, trainer, etc.

Hearing the Mindsets

You can already hear the mindsets of rookies. Most newcomers have the "nobody-somebody" syndrome. They think that if they lose, they'll be nobody. If they win, they'll be somebody. This type of mindset cannot motivate and sustain you. If you constantly need to feed your ego, you're easily derailed by challenges and failures. Superstars are wildly competitive, but their drive does not come from ego. It comes from their desire to give their best in whatever they do.

Major Points

✓ Not all superstars are "naturals".

✓ Think about a sports activity you are not good at. Challenge that belief.

✓ Mental strength and character are more important than talent.

✓ Sometimes, being physically gifted is a curse. Many gifted athletes are not successful because they do not cope well with failure and adversity.

✓ Players with the growth mindset find success in improving, training, and learning. Winning is just a bonus for them.

Chapter 5 – Business: Mindset and Leadership

Enron and the Talent Mindset

Enron Corporation was once the most promising corporation in America. However, in 2001, it was revealed that the company was engaged in accounting fraud now known as the Enron Scandal. What happened? Was it corruption or incompetence? Well, it was mindset.

Malcolm Gladwell once wrote that the United States is obsessed with talent. This type of mindset led to Enron's destruction. The company worshipped talent and made its employees act like they were extraordinarily gifted. This culture pushed the company's employees to hide their deficiencies and mistakes. For people with a fixed mindset, flaws are unacceptable. This kind of thinking pushed company employees to commit fraud.

Organizations that Grow

Jim Collins has studied organizations that have grown significantly in just a few years. He found that the key to a company's growth is its leader. The leaders of growing companies are not charismatic and egomaniac types. They are humble with a great passion for learning. They are not afraid to admit their mistakes and are confident that if they put in the right amount of effort, they will succeed.

They have a growth mindset and believe in the power of human development. These leaders are not trying to prove they are superior and better than others: they are trying to improve themselves. They surround themselves with people smarter than them. They make decisions based on facts and not on a false perception of their intellect and talent.

A Study of Mindset and Management Decisions

A team led by Albert Bandura and Robert Wood conducted research on graduate students with extensive management experience. The researchers gave the students a task of managing a simulated furniture company. They had to make decisions based on given employee productivity data.

The researchers divided the students into two groups: the fixed mindset and the growth mindset. The first group was told that the task was used to measure intelligence. The second group was told that the task was simply an opportunity to develop their skills.

The task was hard; but, the students with the growth mindset just keep on getting better. They kept on learning; they maintained a great sense of confidence despite of constant challenge, pressure, and failure.

Leadership and the Fixed Mindset

Fixed mindset leaders need to constantly affirm their intelligence and talent. They get rid of people who threaten their superiority. They do not build a management team. Instead, they surround themselves with little helpers who feed their egos. It's no surprise that the word "CEO" has been synonymous with "enormous ego". They believe they are superior and display that superiority by hiring minions to feed that need.

Fixed Mindset Leaders in Action

Great leaders are not interested in being a leader. They do not need to prove themselves. They just do what they love with passion and enthusiasm.

Fixed mindset leaders like Lee Iacocca do not have that kind of passion or behavior. They crave approval and affirmation of their superiority. Instead of investing time in developing new cars, Iacocca focused on enhancing his public image. He did not approve new designs because he was afraid that his subordinates would get credit for it.

He became a tyrant, firing people who criticized him. He did not value his employees. He was worried about not being the greatest man in Chrysler. Instead of fighting his competitors head on, he resorted to excuses. He wasted time criticizing his rivals rather than making his company better. He wanted to be the smartest guy in the room. This mindset resulted in the destruction of the company he worked hard to build.

Geniuses like Jerry Levin and Steve Case also almost brought down Time Warner and AOL. They both have an air of supreme talent and intelligence. They do not listen to complaints. They were brutal bosses. Because of the huge ego of these leaders, AOL lost 100 billion dollars in 2002.

Growth Mindset Leaders in Action

Andrew Carnegie said that he wanted to be remembered as the man who hired people who were smarter than he.

The fixed mindset world is small, limiting and confining. But, the growth mindset world is filled with possibilities. It is filled with enthusiasm and energy.

Growth mindset leaders believe in human development. They do not use their company to validate their greatness. They treat their companies as vehicles of development and growth.

Jack Welch of General Electric is a growth mindset leader. When he led GE in the early 1980s, the company was valued at 14 billion dollars. In 2000, the company was valued at 490 billion. Jack was a caring boss. He was nurturing. He hired the right workers and was not threatened by the smart ones. He constantly visited factories. He listened to factory workers. He put emphasis on teamwork. He did not think of himself as a hero or superstar.

He believed that true confidence is being open to change and even criticism. His greatest asset was his readiness to grow. He hired employees based on their mindsets and not skills or talent. He did hire a number of engineers from MIT and

Caltech, but he wanted the ones with an inner hunger. For Welch, GE was all about growth and not self-importance. He got rid of cruel middle managers. He encouraged mentoring as opposed to spreading terror.

Jack Welch had a lot of flaws, but he had a strong desire to grow and be better. He constantly kept his ego in check.

In the 1980s, IBM had a culture of elitism. In 1993, Lou Gestner joined the company as CEO. Gestner changed the company culture. He opened communication channels. He actively attacked the elitist culture and instead promoted an inclusive one. He sent a message that intelligence is not enough: his team had to work hard to get the job done. That's how he saved IBM.

Xerox was in deep trouble when Anne Mulcahy took over in 2000. It was no longer selling copy machines. Then, in 2004, she turned the company around. How did she do it? Well, she and another executive, Ursula Burns, took the time to learn all they had to know about the business. She looked into everything – taxes, debt and inventory. She even worked on weekends.

She was honest and told everyone the truth. Even if the company was struggling financially, she did not retract the employees' annual raise and even gave them birthday leave. She even hosted retirement parties and employee reunions. She wanted to boost the company morale.

After two years, Mulcahy used her growth mindset to transform the company and diversify. Xerox is not strictly a copy machine company anymore. They expanded to mobile, print and business solutions.

A Study of Growth Processes

A researcher named Robert Wood conducted a study focusing on management groups. He formed thirty groups of three people. The members of fifteen groups had a growth mindset while the members of the rest had a fixed mindset.

The groups were tasked to complete a challenging management problem. The fixed mindset groups were told that management skills are something that's fixed – you either have it or you don't. The second group was told that people can always improve their management skills.

The two groups started out with the same abilities. However as time went by, the growth-mindset groups outperformed those with the fixed mindset. Why? Because the members of these groups were honest with each other. They did not try to cover up mistakes. They worked as a team and not as individuals. The fixed mindset groups, on the other hand, did not have open and productive discussions. They had what we call "groupthink".

Groupthink Versus we Think

Groupthink happens when everyone in the group shares the same views. It happens when group members have blind faith in their leaders. It happens when a leader punishes an employee for airing his concern. The group members see their leader as a god who is not capable of making a bad decision. Irving Janis developed this concept in the 1970s and it is often associated with the fixed mindset.

An opposing concept is called "we think". This happens when a leader gives his members rewards for defying him, as David Packard used to do. This concept is often associated with the growth mindset.

The Praised Generation Hits the Workforce

There are a number of parents who shower their kids with praise. They're not to blame. We've been told that praising our children is good for them. But, these praises can turn them into entitled adults. So, what happens when the praised generation or the "Millennials" enter the workforce? Well, leaders must make sure that they praise effort rather than a brilliant performance. This is the only way we can develop a mature workforce.

Are Negotiators Born or Made?

Negotiation is an important business skill. But, like any other business ability, negotiation skill is something you can learn over time. Having a growth mindset makes you want to think "win-win", and this kind of thinking allows you to get other people to "buy in".

Are Managers Made?

Managers are made, not born. All management skills are learnable. Great managers are, surprisingly, those who have a passion for learning and teaching. They are passionate about learning something new. They are also generous enough to teach their subordinates a few tricks. They persevere even when faced with difficult problems.

Grow Your Mindset Tips

Your employees' performance will not improve if you just point out their mistakes. You have to coach them so they can learn from you. You should arrange coaching sessions, trainings and apprenticeships. You should tolerate opposing views and learn to accept constructive criticism. You should inspire your workers to be independent thinkers.

Major Points

✓ The mindset of a company's leader is the key to its growth.

✓ Leaders with a fixed mindset think they have superior talent and intelligence. They will do anything to protect this perception.

✓ Leaders with a fixed mindset do not want to admit their mistakes. They are entitled and surround themselves with flatterers. They become brutal and controlling bosses.

✓ A leader's fixed mindset can cause a company's destruction. It's hard for a fixed mindset organization to keep up with this changing world.

✓ Fixed mindset leaders constantly scream, "Validate me! Affirm me! Worship me!"

✓ Growth mindset leaders do not adopt an elitist company culture. They create an inclusive culture wherein every employee is important.

✓ Growth mindset leaders work hard. They appreciate their employee's efforts.

✓ Not everyone can be a leader; but leaders are made, not born.

✓ Management skills are learnable. Therefore, managers are made, not born.

Chapter 6: Relationships: The Mindsets in Love (or not)

The path to true love is not easy: it is paved with heartbreaks. Fixed mindset people think that rejection means they are unlovable. Instead of moving on, they feel intense sadness and bitterness. They also seek revenge. They have a hard time forgiving those who have hurt their feelings and dignity. But, people with a growth mindset forgive easily. They do not waste time feeling sorry for themselves. They just move on.

Relationships are Different

Benjamin Bloom once conducted research on gifted people – Olympic athletes, pianists, mathematicians, neurologists, etc. But, he did not study people who are gifted in interpersonal relationships because he could not accurately measure social ability. In the next sections of this book, you will discover why some people have the ability to build happy, lasting and fulfilling relationships.

Mindsets Falling in Love

When you have a fixed mindset, you believe that your qualities, your partner's qualities, and relationship components are fixed. If you have a fixed mindset, you'll strive to find the ideal partner – someone who's meant to be with you. A fixed mindset believes that if you have to work at a relationship, it's not meant to be. But, the truth is, people's qualities are not fixed; they can change.

People with a growth mindset do not expect magic and fireworks in a relationship. They believe that a lasting relationship is built through constant effort. The problem is, most relationship experts will tell you that you have to find someone who's perfectly compatible and there should be no effort. Both partners should be able to read each other's mind. But, relationships can only thrive through open communication. To build a lasting relationship, you should try not to make assumptions.

People with a fixed mindset think that relationship problems are signs of personal flaws. When there's a problem, they blame their partner or themselves.

The Partner as Enemy

Most people with a fixed mindset do not want to be seen as the bad guy. They blame their partners when things go wrong. On some days, they see their partners as the lights of their lives. But, on others, they see their partners as the enemy. They sulk in bitterness and hate.

Competition: Who's the Greatest

People with a fixed mindset treat their partners as competitors and not teammates. They feel small when their partners shine brighter. They strive to be the better partner and the more successful one.

Developing Relationships

When you enter into a relationship, you develop a partnership with someone who is different from you. But, even if you are different from your partner, both of you should be on the same side. This is how trust develops.

Friendships

A number of people use their friendships to validate their worth. They use their friends to feel good about themselves. They surround themselves with validators; they feel bad when their friends succeed. These people have a fixed mindset. To form meaningful friendships, you should adopt a growth mindset.

Shyness

Many people use other people to lift themselves up. Shy people are the exact opposite. They are constantly worried about being embarrassed in social situations.

Shyness can hold people back from making new friends or business connections. Research conducted by Jennifer Beer shows that a fixed mindset makes you anxious and self-conscious. It's safe to say that most shy people have a fixed mindset, although there are also a lot of people who have both a growth and fixed mindset.

Shy growth-mindset people look at their shyness as a challenge. So, they try to find ways to manage their nerves. They use coping mechanisms to get themselves to go out and meet new people. They do not allow their shyness to control them: they let go of their fears.

Bullies and Victims: Revenge Visited

Rejection happens all the time in school. Some kids experience bullying at a very early age. They are often tormented and ridiculed even if they did not do anything wrong. This can lead to resentment and depression.

So, what is bullying all about? Well, it's about judging others. More popular kids judge less popular children. They see the misfits as less valuable. Bullies increase their self-esteem when they give the nerds a hard time. They increase their popularity and social status. They become cool and powerful.

Bullies often have a fixed mindset. They believe that some people are superior while others are inferior. They choose people they think are inferior as targets.

Revenge and Bullying Victims

Bullying sometimes leads to depression and suicide. It sometimes leads to violence and revenge. But, sometimes, the victims see bullying as an opportunity to stand up for themselves and make themselves better. How the victims react to bullying depends on their mindset. When the victims feel judged by bullying and rejection, they become bitter and seek revenge.

People with a growth mindset do not see bullying as a reflection of who they are. They see it as the bully's problem. They understand that people bully others to feel good about themselves and elevate their self-esteem. So, instead of seeking revenge, they stand up against their bullies and educate them.

So, what can be done? Well, the schools have to do something to stop bullying. Schools should educate about the different mindsets and encourage kids to adopt the growth mindset.

Major Points

- ✓ People with a growth mindset build lasting and more satisfying relationships.

- ✓ People with a fixed mindset often compete with their partners and use their relationships to validate their worth.

- ✓ To build a happy relationship, you should believe that your partner is capable of changing.

- ✓ Bullies are people who have a fixed mindset. They bully others to build their worth and self-esteem.

- ✓ Victims should not allow bullying to define their value as a human being.

✓ Schools should do something about bullying.

Chapter 7: Parents, Teachers, and Coaches: Where do Mindsets Come From?

Parents generally want to provide their children with all the tools and support they need to succeed in life. And yet, they do things that send a different message.

Fixed mindset parents act like they are judging their kids – either you're good enough or not. They only love their offspring when they meet their terms. They say, "I will only love you if you are successful". But, growth mindset parents show their children that they are interested in their development and not only their output.

Messages About Success and Failure

Many parents and teachers tell their kids/students, "You are intelligent because you're a fast learner". They say something like, "You got great scores even if you're not studying". Most parents think these messages boost kids' self-esteem. But, they hear a different message. They think that if they are not fast learners, they're not smart. They think that if they have to study to get good scores, they are not good enough.

Children love praise and it increases their self-esteem. But, if they fail, their self-confidence can easily reach rock bottom. So, should you stop praising your kids? No. Instead of praising intelligence or talent, laud them for their persistence, effort and doing their best. This will encourage them to try harder, persevere and study more.

Refrain from saying things like "you're stupid" or "you're clumsy" to your kids. Do not punish them for not doing well in school or screwing something up. When your kids drop something, just tell them to pick it up. Train them to look for solutions and solve their problems. When they fail, tell them the truth and teach them how to turn that failure around.

What Makes a Great Teacher or Parent?

Many parents and teachers think that lowering their standards increases their children's achievement and self-esteem. To the contrary, lowering standards leads to easy success. The best way to maximize a child's potential is to raise the standards and then provide the tools and necessary training to meet them.

Great teachers are fascinated with the learning process and human development. They believe that anyone can increase their abilities. Great teachers do not give up on their students even if they do not want to learn. They strive to learn along with their students. Amazing teachers are not interested in teaching: they are interested in learning. When teachers are judging students, they will get back at the teachers by not trying.

Coaches: Winning Through Mindset

Having a fixed mindset makes you judgmental. It makes you incapable of admitting and accepting failure. Bobby Knight was a famous coach. He could be kind, but he could also be cruel. He could not take failure and yelled at his players when things did not go his way. He motivated players by humiliating them. The coach's cruelty destroyed some of the best players. But, Steve Alford did not allow the yelling to get to him. He stayed optimistic even when the environment was poisonous. Knight believed in the capacity of his players to develop. But, he thought that his ability as a coach was fixed, so, he gave up when things did not go his way.

When John Wooden, the great basketball coach, first worked at UCLA, the university did not have a good place where players could practice. Plus, the players were really bad. But, the coach did not give up. He was wise and believed that his team could get better. He constantly trained the players to improve their dribbling and shooting skills. He conditioned them and gave them the right mindset.

After a few years, the UCLA basketball team became one of the best college teams in the United States. He found the holy grail of success – full preparation and maximum effort. He pushed the players to give one hundred percent. He didn't ask his team not to fail. He asked them to give their best effort. He gave equal attention to every players. He taught his players not to let success or failure get into their heads.

Our Legacy

As parents, coaches and teachers, we have the responsibility to make sure that our children, students and athletes adopt a growth mindset. This is the key to fulfilling our mission of helping these kids reach their full potential.

Major Points

✓ The Holy Grail to success is full effort and preparation.

✓ Beware of success because it makes you sloppy.

✓ Great teachers put a premium on effort. They push their students to give tone hundred percent all the time. They do not give up on their students.

✓ Praise your child's efforts, not results.

Chapter 8: Changing Mindsets

The main premise of the growth mindset is that anyone can change. This chapter is about how we can change our mindsets.

The Nature of Change

In life, there are a number of bright and talented people unable to cope with challenges and adversities. They do not take action to make things better. They feel powerless when things go wrong.

The truth is that your beliefs are the key to your misery or happiness. We are constantly monitoring and interpreting what happens to us. But, people with a fixed mindset make exaggerated interpretations and then react with superiority, anger or depression.

Fixed mindset people run accounts of what happens to them and then draw conclusions like:

- This means that I am better.

- This means that I am not a good spouse.

- This means that I will not succeed in life.

When something good happens to a fixed mindset person, he exaggerates his self-worth. When something bad happens, he intensely devalues his worth.

People with a growth mindset do not judge themselves. When they fail, they ask questions like "how can I learn from this?", "how can I improve?", or "how can I help my spouse?"

To change your mindset, you have to challenge your conclusions and focus on what you can learn from the situation.

The next sections of this chapter will help you silence your inner critic and develop a strong growth mindset.

The Mindset Lectures

The mere understanding of the two mindsets can significantly change your life. Let's look at the case of Maggie, a budding writer. Whenever she writes, she hears herself say, "Don't do it" or "Do not share your writing and embarrass yourself." After taking Dr. Dweck's mindset class, her inner voice now tells her to go for it and chase her dreams.

Jason was an athlete. Before he attended Dr. Dweck's class, his inner voice always told him that he has to win. Now, his inner voice is telling him to learn, improve and become better.

Tony, a genius, used to hear a voice that says, "I am a genius and I am better than others. I do not need to study." Then, when he failed, he used to hear a voice that said, "I am losing my gift". After understanding the two mindsets, he now hears a voice that says, "Do not worry about failures, they're normal. You do not have to know everything."

Sticking to the growth mindset is not always easy. Sometimes, we just want to sulk over our defeats. But, having a growth mindset takes you out of the fantasy that you are a genius, an amazing writer, or an amazing athlete so you will exert the effort to transform these fantasies into reality.

Attending a growth mindset workshop can make a great impact on your life. It helps you understand the truth that to achieve something great, you must be willing to do the extra work.

Brainology

Dr. Dweck and her team developed the Brainology program, an animated program that helps students understand that even cool kids and geniuses encounter problems and failures. The program contains study and problem-solving strategies. After taking the program, the students' grades improved. The teachers also changed their ways: they learned a lot about themselves.

More About Change

If Carol Dweck's programs brought significant change in the lives of her students, is it therefore that easy to change?

Well, fixed mindset people hold on to their beliefs because it serves them at some point in their lives. This mindset tells them that they are who they want to be. It helps them increase their self-esteem and gain the love of people who matter to them.

It's hard to give up a fixed mindset because it means that you have to give up the beliefs that have helped elevate your self-esteem. It forces you to give up the idea that you are better or smarter than others. You fear that you'll lose your identity and become ordinary.

Taking the First Step

Imagine that you have applied to a prestigious graduate school. You are confident that you will get in, but the school has rejected your application. Your fixed mindset voice would tell you that you are not good enough or worthy to get in. Then, you'd say an affirmation to regain your self-esteem. For most people, it stops here. But, to develop the growth mindset, you have to move on to the self-development part.

To do this, think about your goal of getting into that university. What are the things you need to do to fulfill it? What is the school looking for? What do you need to do for your next application? What can you learn from this experience? You should create a concrete plan on how you can improve yourself and reach your goal. This plan will increase your chances of achieving the goal.

Let's say, you took the step to make yourself better, but you still failed. Now what would you do? Well, you just have to pick yourself up again and repeat the process. Learn from the experience. Make yourself better.

Now, imagine that you are a promising quarterback. You always win and are the top pick of a national football team. The problem is that you now feel the pressure. You are playing with players who are better and more experienced than you.

If you have a fixed mindset, you'll most likely torture yourself. You get humiliated each time you fail and do not live up to expectations.

But, if you have a growth mindset, you acknowledge your failure. You also tell yourself that you are adjusting. You do whatever you can to learn. You spend time with more experienced quarterbacks and ask for help. You practice and give your one hundred percent every game. You work hard: you do your part as a team member.

People Who Don't Want Change

There are people who don't want to change. They are so entitled that they think the world owes them something. They feel they deserve a better life, house or a car without putting in any effort.

Now, let's say that you are underpaid. You feel that your talent is not recognized. Your boss thinks you have an attitude problem. If you have a fixed mindset, you'll think that your boss is threatened by your talent. You don't feel that there's a need to change.

To change your mindset, you have to give up the idea that you are superior. You have to understand that people stand out because of their effort. So, you work harder. It will take a while before you enjoy putting in a lot of it; but, as you become a growth mindset person, people will start to help and support you.

Changing Your Child's Mindset

If your kid has a fixed mindset, he or she will try to avoid failure. He or she might start cheating to cover weaknesses. He thinks that he is better than everyone else and doesn't have to put in effort.

How do you change a child's mindset? Talking him or her into the growth mindset doesn't work. You have to live it. After school, ask your offspring what he or she learned. Encourage him or her to be honest about mistakes and ask how he or she can learn from them.

Praise improvement. Encourage him or to talk about the things learned. Teach your child to find joy in solving complicated problems. You want to let your child know that an intellectual gift is not everything you care about. You want him or her to know that effort matters, too.

The fixed mindset is alluring because it promises kids that they will have a life of success and glory. But, it's not true. The real world is filled with challenges and they will fail many times before they achieve success.

You also need to be careful about how you praise hard work. Sometimes, children putting in too much effort can become a problem. Some might get sick from putting too much effort. How do you prevent this from happening and still maintain your child's growth mindset? You have to allow your child to enjoy what he or she does. You should train him or her to find joy in studying or taking piano lessons. Praise your child's effort, but do not exert pressure.

Mindset and Willpower

Fixed mindset individuals think that people who have willpower are strong. They believe that those who do not have it are weak. This is why they beat themselves up when they break their diets or lose control over their emotions.

To strengthen your willpower, you have to discover the strategies that work for you and practice them constantly. If something doesn't work, change your technique.

Maintaining Change

Changing something is easier than maintaining change. People stop eating healthy once they lose that extra weight. But, this is not how growth works. Changing your mindset is not just about learning a few tricks: it's about changing how you think. It is about seeing things with new eyes. You must commit yourself to changing your mindset and keep trying. You should surround yourself with people who support you.

The Road Ahead

Change is tough, but in the end, it's worth it. Having a growth mindset does not eliminate all your problems and challenges. But, it makes your life better.

Major Points

✓ You can change your mindset.

✓ To change your mindset, you should change the way you think. You should focus on learning from your mistakes.

✓ To change your child's mindset, you have to praise effort and emphasize the importance of the learning process.

Conclusion

Thank you for downloading this book. I hope that you've already gained a clear understanding of the two mindsets. I hope that, at this point, you are already getting ready to drop your fixed mindset and adopt a growth one.

In Chapter 1, we learned what the growth mindset is and how it's different from the fixed mindset. The fixed mindset is the belief that everyone has a fixed amount of intelligence: you are either smart or stupid. The growth mindset is the belief that everyone can be good at something with effort and constant practice.

In Chapter 2, we had an in-depth discussion of the two mindsets. We discussed the dangers of the CEO disease or having a huge ego. Being too proud will get in the way of your growth: it can make you lazy. If you have a growth mindset, you will not take criticism to heart. You'll just use it to get better at what you do.

In Chapter 3, we learned that ability does not guarantee success or achievement. There's no such thing as intellectual gift. Intelligent people are just individuals who have a heightened curiosity and a strong passion for learning. Most skills can be learned through constant practice. We have discussed how positive labels can destroy you and keep you from achieving everything you want in life. When people call you smart, you will not take risks. You'll stay away from challenging tasks to protect your ego and pride.

In Chapter 4, we entered into the world of sports. Stars are made and not born. Michael Jordan was not born special: he was persistent. He practiced day and night. In this chapter, we defined success as putting forth your best effort.

In Chapter 5, we discussed how the mindset of a corporate leader can lead to the company's success or failure. Fixed mindset leaders will do anything to cover their mistakes. Growth mindset leaders are not afraid to admit them. They're grounded and don't believe that they're the smartest people in the room.

In Chapter 6, we discussed how having a fixed mindset can destroy relationships. To have a harmonious relationship with your partner, you have to believe that he or she can change. In this chapter, we also examined the psyche of bullies – people who put others down to feel good about themselves.

In Chapter 7, we discussed the effect of parents and teachers on a child's mindset. Great teachers do not judge students.

They teach them, give them feedback, and show them how it's done. They praise efforts and not results.

In Chapter 8, we discussed how we can change our mindset. Adopting the growth mindset is not as hard as you may think. You have to believe that you can learn just about anything. You have to drop the perception that you are better than others. You have to stop looking for external validation and start competing against your past self.

Having a growth mindset can do wonders in your life. It can make you become more persistent, reliable and likable. Most importantly, it brings you closer to success.

FREE BONUSES

P.S. Is it okay if we overdeliver?

Here at Readtrepreneur Publishing, we believe in overdelivering way beyond our reader's expectations. Is it okay if we overdeliver?

Here's the deal, we're going to give you an extremely condensed PDF summary of the book which you've just read and much more…

What's the catch? We need to trust you… You see, we want to overdeliver and in order for us to do that, we've to trust our reader to keep this bonus a secret to themselves? Why? Because we don't want people to be getting our exclusive PDF summaries even without buying our books itself. Unethical, right?

Ok. Are you ready?

Firstly, remember that your book is code: "**READ59**".

Next, visit this link: **http://bit.ly/exclusivepdfs**

Everything else will be self explanatory after you've visited: **http://bit.ly/exclusivepdfs**.

We hope you'll enjoy our free bonuses as much as we enjoyed preparing it for you!

Printed in July 2019
by Rotomail Italia S.p.A., Vignate (MI) - Italy